Up to There in Alligators

More Cartoons by Pat Oliphant

Andrews, McMeel & Parker
A Universal Press Syndicate Affiliate
Kansas City • New York

FOR JIM DECKER
who is responsible, or to
blame, for everything.

Foreword

The first time I remember laughing over one of my old man's cartoons I was about ten years old. The arrival of the evening's *Denver Post* was always an event around our place. My mother, my older sister, family friends, whoever was around would laugh appreciatively after looking over the day's Oliphant, and I'd jump in with a stupid consensual grin on my face secretly wondering why it just didn't seem as funny as Peanuts. One day, I decided that as the chip off the old block I should at least feign understanding by laughing first, and so I retrieved the paper, opened it to the editorial page, and laughed the most appreciative laugh that a ten-year-old boy can muster, which, I recall red-faced, is a damned impressive high-pitched squeal. So there I was, laughing what I thought must surely be the most intelligent laugh that I had ever laughed, everyone crowding around to see the "good one" my dad had gotten off, and then silence. No clan participation in the general hilarity of adult intellectual perspicacity; just puzzled looks, grim even. I was laughing at a caricature of Uncle Sam welcoming his dead boys home from Vietnam.

Yes, I felt like an idiot (and my old man will no doubt construe it as proof positive that I was destined for a career as an editor, for which profession he has only the highest regard), but I feel less foolish for the company I keep. My father has made an art of blasting his readers — from his ten-year-old son to the nation's leaders — out of our safe expectations. And that, I am convinced, is what makes him the best in his profession.

He does it by following two seemingly obvious golden rules. The first is one that is completely lost on the incestuous, back-slapping denizens of our nation's capital: Don't fraternize with the folks you lampoon. As a kid, I was impressed whenever a letter from a politician or even the White House arrived, but these always ended up haphazardly strewn in boxes or tossed in storage. It was the letters from angry average readers that were pinned up in the studio or responded to, even if only with the word "Bullshit!" stamped all over them. It is those people Pat Oliphant wants to reach; playing savior to our politicians he leaves to the amorphous "thought leaders" who have long since lost their edge.

His second golden rule is even tougher: Hard work. One comment you get all the time as the son of a cartoonist is, "Gee, your dad gets to do that for a living?" Or, "It must be nice to be so talented and have a job like that." I suspect it is. But while talent is nine-tenths of the equation, that last tenth is something that to this day my dad doesn't take for granted. The breadth of his knowledge on the art of cartooning, everything from technique to style to history, is astounding. Many of his contemporaries resent his gruff dismissal of their work, but what they might be surprised to discover is that he knows more about their style than they do themselves.

Whatever the explanation, folks love him for it, if only because he delivers gut-wrenching blows on subjects that our "Entertainment Tonight" society can make us forget we care about. To be honest, there's a little bit of Annie Wilkes in all of us. Like the "Number One Fan" of Stephen King's creation, we all like this Oliphant guy just the way he is, except maybe he could be just a bit nicer to (pick your favorite sensitivity group) the military, women, Italians, Catholics, Jews, evangelicals, postal workers, patriots, Arabs, blacks, politicians, kids, homosexuals, editors, and so on. But then we'd have either the partisan peanut brittle or the mashed-potato commentary glop we get dished up elsewhere, and fortunately for all of us, this cartoonist doesn't work that way.

I suppose every son wants to be able to say his dad's the best. But if you check out this collection, I think you'll agree that my old man is indeed all right.

GRANT OLIPHANT

Grant Oliphant is editor of the magazine American Politics *in Washington, D.C., a publication which uses the work of far too many other cartoonists on its pages. I have spoken to the lad firmly about this, but appear to have no influence. He is also co-host of "The Power Breakfast," a daily morning radio talk show, dealing with politics and social issues.*

I wonder could I cartoon for radio . . .

Pat O.

June 1, 1986

'YOUR PAPERS APPEAR TO BE IN ORDER. APPARENTLY YOU ARE A HETEROSEXUAL MARRIED COUPLE. SORRY, WE THOUGHT YOU MIGHT BE A COUPLA QUEERS.'

5

Papa knows best.*

*This and all other postscripts by Pat Oliphant.

At last, a tax bill.

June 9, 1986

WALDHEIM ÜBER ALLES

Austria's Kurt Waldheim wins the election despite his history as a Nazi
in World War II. Or perhaps *because* of it.

'IF WE HAD THIS FIGHT ALL FIXED, WHAT'S BURGER DOING OVER IN *THAT* CORNER?'

'YOU'RE ALL UNDER ARREST!'

Apartheid in South Africa. Piet Botha doesn't fool around.

Rehnquist and Scalia nominated to the Supreme Court.

One never can tell who he'll run into down the road, however.

June 26, 1986

HOUSE MEMBERS CHECKING THEIR VERTEBRAL COLUMNS BEFORE DOING BATTLE WITH THE PRESIDENT ON CONTRA AID IN NICARAGUA.

14

'OK, FIREBOATS — ON MY SIGNAL, WET THE T-SHIRT!'

Getting ready for the Statue's 100th birthday.

July 7, 1986

July 9, 1986

18

'DON'T CRY. MR. ROZELLE JUST WANTS TO TEST YOU FOR DRUG USE. EVERYONE WILL GET TESTED FOR DRUG USE. NOW, C'MON — GIVE MR. ROZELLE A SPECIMEN.'

July 11, 1986

'NOT TONIGHT, DEAR — IT'S PROBABLY ILLEGAL.'

20

Her Royal Highness and Her Magginess express themselves.

AT LAST, A COHERENT POLICY ON SOUTH AFRICA. AND IN RESPONSE, THE REPUBLICAN WOMEN OF AMERICA EAGERLY TURN IN THEIR PRECIOUS BAUBLES.

24   White House Chief of Staff Regan observes that American women will not take kindly to the side-effects of sanctions against South Africa — notably an increase in the price of gold and diamonds.

LET THE HEARINGS COMMENCE

The Chief-Justice-to-be begins his confirmation hearings.

A THIRD TERM FOR REAGAN? HEY, I'LL DRINK TO THAT!'

The Rehnquist hearings continue.
Interesting real estate data from another era surface.

Tough times demand tough action.

A DEAL

The Oil Brothers together again.

"...NOW, WITH HIS WIFE'S ENCOURAGEMENT, MR. WYETH IS TACKLING NEW SUBJECTS."

All America is titillated by Mr. Wyeth's nude Helga pictures.
As America would be.

THE SMOKER'S SEAT.

Déjà vu — old names and new places.

And after it all, the Chief Justice is confirmed.

Happy parents, Rep. Dan Rostenkowski and Sen. Robert Packwood.

New York Times correspondent framed in Moscow.

Inept flying schools, airline deregulation, a shortage of air traffic
controllers . . . a deadly mix.

Harvard celebrates a birthday.

Changes and cutbacks in the Golden World of Television.

'WHAT THE HELL WAS ALL THAT ABOUT?'

Chief Justice Rehnquist, and baggage.

'I'M DISGUSTED WITH REAGAN FOR CAVING IN TO THE RUSSIANS OVER DANILOFF
— BUT I **LOVE** THE WAY THE RUSSIANS TREAT THE PRESS!'

45

TV preacher declares for presidency. God impressed.

'WELL, GOLLY, HERE I AM IN MY OWN WONDERFUL NEW JIMMY CARTER PRESIDENTIAL CENTER ... I WONDER IF ANYONE WILL EVER COME VISIT.'

The Killer Rabbit Who Wouldn't Die.

Japan's leader declares that the industrial progress of the U.S. is held
back by its mixed racial background.

The end of a less than perfect Summit.

THE VIGIL — ELIE WIESEL, NOBEL PEACE PRIZE, 1986.

'WHERE DO YOU STAND ON DEFENDING AMERICA?'

Another presidential buzz-term.

Mr. Hasenfus, a hapless gunrunner's assistant whom nobody ever heard of, including his employers, is captured when his plane crashes in Nicaragua.

51

'HI, THIS IS RONALD REAGAN, AND I WANT TO ASK YOU, "ARE YOU ANY BETTER OFF TODAY THAN YOU WERE FOUR YEARS AGO?"...'

DIPLOMATIC EXCHANGES.

TRICK OR TREAT?

Halloween.

He said *something* at Reykjavik.

Fall campaigning — personalities instead of issues.

November 3, 1986

'LOOK, TAKE HIM HOME AND TRY HIM OUT FOR A TERM, IF IT DOESN'T WORK OUT, BRING HIM BACK.'

57

Non-AKC, not spayed, possibly rabid. But cute.

November 6, 1986

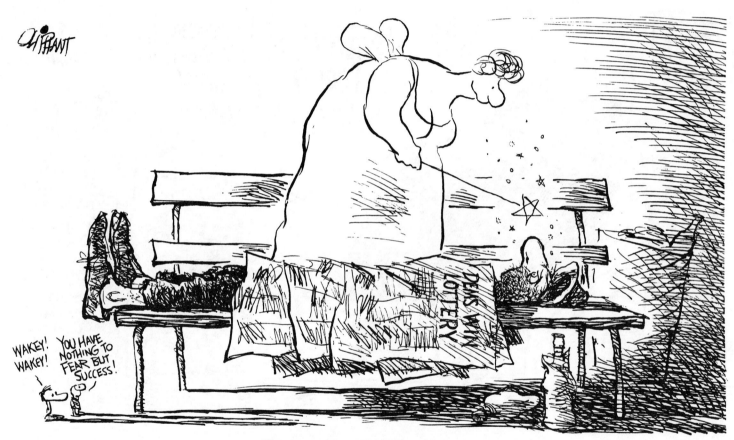

DEMOCRAT DAWNING

Democrats win election successes . . .

. . . TV preacher does not.

'I SHOULDN'T REALLY BE DOING THIS — I'LL HAVE TO TRUST YOU TO KEEP IT QUIET.'

'WHEN THE COMPLETE IRAN STORY IS TOLD, YOU'LL ALL UNDERSTAND.'

November 18, 1986

THE REAGAN GANG — 'CREEPS' CASEY, 'BUGS' BUCHANAN, BOBBY 'THE CAKE' MⴤFARLANE,
THE BOSS, JOHN 'THE ADMIRAL' POINDEXTER AND 'RATS' REGAN — WITH HOSTAGE.

STANDING SMALL

In the wake of all the brave John Wayne talk . . .

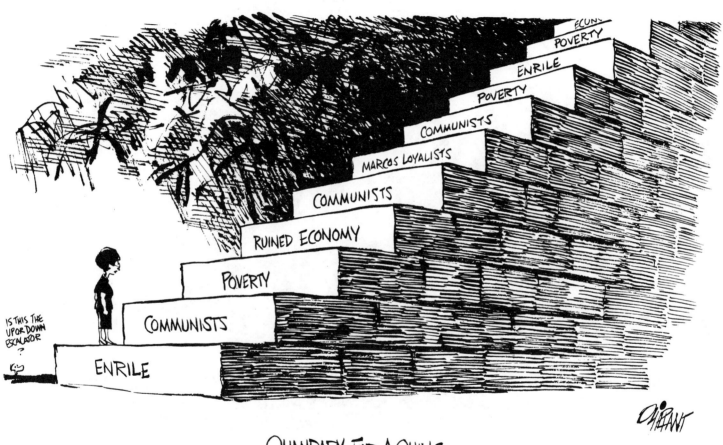

QUANDARY FOR AQUINO.

'I DON'T MAKE MISTAKES. JOHN POINDEXTER MAKES MISTAKES. OLIVER NORTH MAKES MISTAKES. ISRAEL MAKES MISTAKES. SAUDI ARABIA MAKES MISTAKES...'

Ayatollah Reagan with mullahs Casey and Regan.

THE PRESIDENT'S ADVISER.

The power behind the throne.

December 2, 1986

You mean, life *is* like the movies?

December 11, 1986

A NEW YORK BUSINESSMAN INFORMS CIA DIRECTOR CASEY OF THE
IRANSCAM-CANADA CONNECTION.

That's what Casey claimed — the where and who is conjecture, but
probably accurate, given this administration.

'Tis approaching Christmas. The homeless gather in Lafayette Park.
In the background are North and Poindexter, already "retired"
from the White House.

The president's mind. Or minds.

MOMENTS OF THE DAY WHEN YOU'D REALLY RATHER NOT HEAR ABOUT THE PRESIDENT.

More great moments on TV. The president has prostate surgery.

'HOW DO YOU LIKE THAT? I CAUGHT HIM FLYING IN WAR TOYS FOR THE KIDS!'

Santa Claus in the Hasenfus pose.

December 23, 1986

'INCOMING.'

'I THOUGHT I MIGHT DROP OVER TO PALM SPRINGS FOR A FEW DAYS, LIE AROUND IN THE SUN FOR A BIT, DO A LITTLE RIDING, MAYBE ... BUT THEN I SAID, THE HELL WITH IT.'

The president is at the ranch again.

. . . and a new set of tax laws.

THE DEMOCRAT-CONTROLLED CONGRESS RETURNS...

'THE SURROGATE MOTHER SENT IT OVER FOR YOUR APPROVAL. THE SURROGATE MOTHER SAYS IT IS NOW YOUR RESPONSIBILITY ANYWAY, AND HE DOES NOT WANT IT BACK. SIGN HERE.'

Colonel North takes the fifth.

The Iran-Contra arms deal. Millions of dollars are unaccounted for.

Presidential aide, Patrick Buchanan, is leaving the White House, perhaps
to prime himself for other things.

'WHERE DID WE GO WRONG?'

Chinese students demonstrate for greater social freedom.

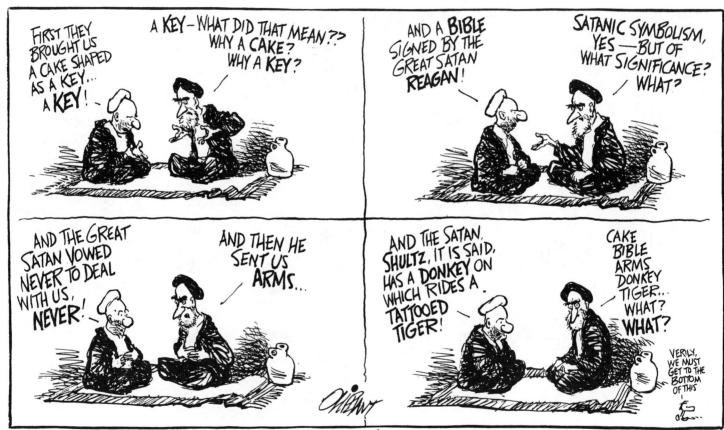

... AND YOU THINK YOU'RE CONFUSED.

Secretary of State Charles Shultz, it is reported by those who should know, sports on his backside a tattoo of a tiger. Such trivia increases the confusion in some people's minds.

Meese and the rights of the accused.

STATE OF THE UNION (ABRIDGED, ANNOTATED, REVISED)

'NO, UNCLE, I KNOW I SHOULDN'T BE HERE... I KNOW I'M A STUPID, SELF-SERVING CLOWN, UNCLE... ANYHOW, UNCLE, WOULD YOU PLEASE PUT THE ENTIRE NATION AT RISK, AND GET ME OUT OF BEIRUT?'

Many of the hostages were in the area in the first place
on missions of tax-free greed.

'WELL, I MUST BE RUNNING ALONG — ENJOY THE FLOWERS!'

The Marcoses continue to smolder in exile.

February 3, 1987

'BUCHANAN'S LEAVING THE SHIP, SIR — I GUESS THAT LEAVES YOU AND ME.'

'YOU WILL HAVE NO MEMORY OF HOW WE TOOK OUR PAY RAISE. YOU WILL FORGET YOU WERE MUGGED BY YOUR CONGRESSMEN. YOU WILL RECALL ONLY MAKING A CHARITABLE CONTRIBUTION...'

February 9, 1987

'FIRST, HE WOKE UP IN THE MIDDLE OF THE SERVICE TO FIND THAT THE SERMON WAS ABOUT AIDS, THEN YOU STARTED PASSING OUT CONDOMS, AND MR. OGILTHORPE BECAME DISORIENTED.'

'WE'RE FEELING GOOD AGAIN ABOUT BEING RUSSIANS. RUSSIA IS STANDING TALL. IT'S MORNING IN THE U.S.S.R. THE NEW OPEN-NESS. WOW!'

Glasnost in progress.

THE PRESIDENT COOPERATES

The three-man Tower Commission questions the president in private
concerning his possible role in the Iran-Contra scandal.

'GOLDMAN, SKINNER AND LYNCH, INSIDER TRADING DIVISION.'

Trouble on Wall Street.

What? Israel? Who, us?

February 18, 1987

STEALTHILY OCCUPYING THE NATION OF ZOMBIES WHILE THEY WATCHED A MINDLESS MINI-SERIES, IVANOVICH STARED A MOMENT TOO LONG AT THE TELEVISION SCREEN...

The mindless mini-series concerned a Soviet takeover of the U.S.

'THAT MRS. REAGAN — HEH, HEH — BOY, WHAT A KIDDER!!'

Reportedly, Mrs. Reagan didn't like Donald Regan, the White House
Chief of Staff, very much at all.

Regan leaves. Reagan expresses regret.

Nancy Is Very Protective of Ronald. PG (language)

THE NEW DIRECTOR

A new Chief of Staff.

EDUCATION IN ALABAMA: FUNDAMENTALISM 101.

Alabama decides to teach the Bible's version of creation alongside
the theory of evolution.

March 9, 1987

'PARDON ME, BUT ARE YOU A CELEBRITY DEMONSTRATING THE PLIGHT OF THE HOMELESS, OR ARE YOU JUST ANOTHER BUM ON A STEAM GRATE?'

Celebrity film stars, etc., steam for a night in Washington.
They know they can always go home.

The CBS strike.

'HEY, NO WAY — I GRANT YOU SPECIAL DISPENSATION, AND I'LL HAVE TO GRANT IT TO EVERYONE!'

THE WRITING OF FORM W·4 XXVII

The new tax form (revised revision).

March 17, 1987

The Editors
The Wall Stweet Journal

Sirs:
In weplying to the wecent scuwwilous attacks upon me
wegarding my actions in cawwying messages fwom Mr.
Ghorbanifar, the arms middleman, to Pwesident Weagan
during the Iwan Arms Cwisis, let me pwotest the
weckless diswegard some cowwespondents seem to have
for my woyal status in the pwess world. We all know
Mr. Ghorbanifar is a wuthless wogue, and I find it
extweemely embawwassing to my weputation to be winked
with him in this wegard. We of the multi-million dollar
pwess cannot be held to such wigid wules which would
pwevent us fwom serving our Pwesident and Countwy.
We are beyond this silly wecwimination and wepwoach.
Wemember, we too, are Amewicans!
I twust you will wemedy the situation and pwevent a
wecuwwence of this wuthless hounding of the Media
by the media.

                    Wespectfully yours,

                    Barbara Wa Wa

P.S. I only hope my pubwic will understand.

SUCH A DEAL.

March 24, 1987

'NOW AURELATE THE FOLLOWING CAVEAT. AL HAIG IS IN COMMAND HERE, AND DON'T YOU OMIT TO COMMIT THAT TO FULL RECALL, NINETEEN EIGHTY EIGHT-WISE!'

Haig announces for '88.

A new speed limit? Only a drunk would drive straight on these highways.

'THE SUPREME COURT SAYS YOUR 20 YEARS EXPERIENCE AND SENIORITY HAS NOTHING TO DO WITH IT, LESTER. THE SUPREME COURT HAS GIVEN YOUR JOB TO MIZ DIMBROWSKI, HERE.'

Affirmative Action at work.

March 30, 1987

PEOPLE IN GLASNOSTS...

Maggie meets Mikhail.

Embassy guards seduced by Soviet operatives.

A slight variation on the Oral Roberts Godscam.

The Surrogate Mother custody ruling.

April 13, 1987

'WHY, HERE'S AN INTERESTING LITTLE TOP-SECRET COMMUNIQUE, JUST IN — THE PRESIDENT HAS OUTLAWED THE SOVIET UNION. WE START BOMBING IN FIVE MINUTES.'

Shultz visits the compromised U.S. Embassy in Moscow.

But more of Mr. Murphy later . . .

Days of deregulation.

'NOT A HEAVYWEIGHT IN THE JOINT!'

When you're young, and lonely, and far from home . . .

FCC RADIO POLICE TODAY ARRESTED SURGEON·GENERAL KOOP FOR BROADCASTING AIDS WARNINGS WHICH CONTAINED SEXUAL INNUENDO.

Space Defense Initiative — an idea ahead of its technology.

'HEY, CUTIE—TELL 'EM YOUR IDEAS FOR GETTING THE NATION OUT OF DEBT!'

'HEY, YOU GUYS—DO WE KNOW ANYONE WHO WEARS SANDALS AND CARRIES A WHIP?'

It couldn't happen to a nicer bunch of guys.

What he means is, "It won't float."

April 30, 1987

GEPHARDT'S TIGER.

149

May 1, 1987

HOME IS THE GARBAGE, HOME FROM THE SEA...

A garbage scow from New York wanders the world in search of a home.

Mr. Murphy's Law catches up with Gary Hart.

Gary Hart and Donna Rice, Meese and Wedtech.

'A PLUS! – NAME RECOGNITION IS **UP**!'

A campaign ends.

'ANYBODY GOT ANY BRILLIANT IDEAS?'

Now, who?

Klaus Barbie goes on trial in France.

May 13, 1987

'10 MILLION DOLLARS DEPOSITED IN OUR SWISS BANK ACCOUNT? THAT DOPEY OLLIE NORTH MUST'VE SCREWED UP AGAIN.'

May 14, 1987

159

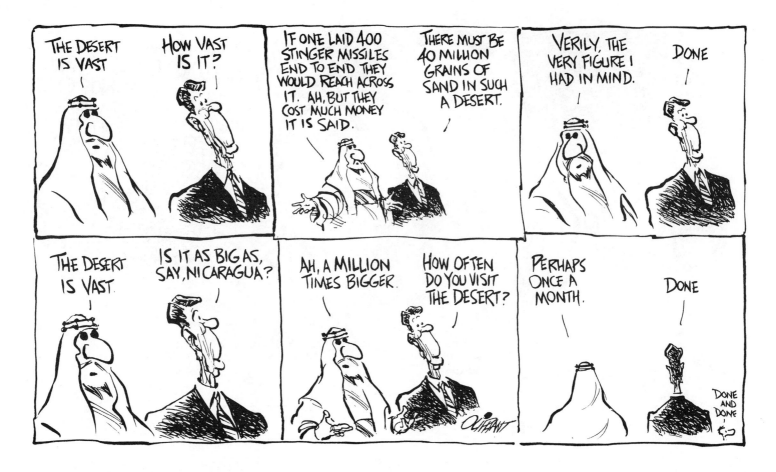

The president and the Saudis have a conversation. Nothing of substance involving U.S. missiles, in exchange for monthly aid to the Nicaraguan Contras, is discussed.

The New York garbage barge, still wandering, still homeless.

May 20, 1987

162

U.S. Navy vessel *Stark* struck by Exocet missile in Persian Gulf.

YOUR TAXES AT WORK.

Pentagon waste struck by Exocet missile in Persian Gulf.

In the year of the 200th anniversary of the Constitution.

HOLY WARS.

May 29, 1987

As protection, oil carriers of other nations to sail under U.S. flag
in the Persian Gulf.

Young German pilot flies Cessna into Moscow's Red Square.

June 2, 1987

Should there or should there not be AIDS testing?

Volcker leaves.

A sneering, arrogant Elliott Abrams testifies on Iran-Contra Investigation.

She can have her childhood later.

Farewell Fred Astaire.